LIFE CYCLES

The Life Cycle of Fish

Darlene R. Stille

Heinemann
LIBRARY

Chicago, Illinois

www.heinemannraintree.com
Visit our website to find out more information about Heinemann-Raintree books.

To order:
☎ Phone 888-454-2279
💻 Visit www.heinemannraintree.com to browse our catalog and order online.

© 2012 Heinemann Library
an imprint of Capstone Global Library, LLC
Chicago, Illinois

Edited by Abby Colich, Megan Cotugno, and Kate deVilliers
Designed by Victoria Allen
Illustrated by Darren Lingard
Picture research by Ruth Blair
Originated by Capstone Global Library, Ltd.
Printed and bound in China by CTPS

14 13 12 11 10
10 9 8 7 6 5 4 3 2 1

Library of Congress Cataloging-in-Publication Data
Stille, Darlene R.
    The life cycle of fish / Darlene Ruth Stille.
        p. cm.—(Life cycles)
    Includes bibliographical references and index.
    ISBN 978-1-4329-4980-8 (hc)—ISBN 978-1-4329-4987-7
(pb) 1. Fishes—Life cycles—Juvenile literature. I. Title.
    QL617.2.S715 2012
    597.156—dc22   2010038278

Acknowledgments
The author and publisher are grateful to the following for permission to reproduce copyright material: © Alamy: pp. 13 (© Visual&Written SL), 26 (© Ross Armstrong), 34 (© Alex Segre); © Corbis: pp. 11 (© Visuals Unlimited), 25 (© Keren Su), 36 (© Daniel Gotshall/Visuals Unlimited), 37 (© Michele Westmorland/Science Faction), 38 (© Specialist Stock); © FLPA: p. 20 (Flip Nicklin/Minden Pictures); © Nature PL: pp. 22 (© DOC WHITE), 43 (© Doug Perrine); © Photolibrary: pp. 6 (Peter Arnold images/Doug Perrine), 10, 14 (age fotostock/Marevision),15 (age fotostock/Marevision), 17 (Animals Animals/ER Degginger), 21 (age fotostock/Morales), 23 (OSF), 24 (age fotostock/Marevision), 27 (OSF/Alan and Joan Root), 30 (BSIP Medical/GUILLAUMIN), 40 (Alaska Stock Images); © Shutterstock: pp. 4 (© Pinosub), 7 (© Rich Carey), 12 (© Hugh Lansdown), 19 (© Stubblefield Photography), 28 (© Kpegg), 29 (© tubuceo), 32 (© oksana.perkins), 33 (© Eric Gevaert), 35 (© Konstantin Ovchinnikov), 39 (© Eugene Sim), 41 (© Anson0618).

Cover photograph of the Spine Cheek Anenomefish in Indonesia, reproduced with permission of © Photolibrary (WaterFrame - Underwater Images/Rodger Klein).

We would like to thank Dr. Michael Bright for his invaluable help in the preparation of this book.

Every effort has been made to contact copyright holders of any material reproduced in this book. Any omissions will be rectified in subsequent printings if notice is given to the publisher.

Contents

Some words are shown in bold, **like this**. You can find out what they mean by looking in the glossary.

Look but don't touch: Many fish are easily hurt. If you see one in the wild, do not get too close to it. Look at it, but do not try to touch it!

What Is a Fish?

Fish come in an awesome variety of sizes, shapes, and colors. So what makes a fish, a fish?

Traits of all fish

All fish have several characteristics, or traits, in common. Most fish live in water and breathe through **gills**. Like animals that live on land, fish need a gas called **oxygen** to live. Land animals have organs called **lungs** that take in oxygen from the air. Fish do not have lungs. They take oxygen from water with their gills.

How Do Gills Work?

A fish breathes as it swims. Water flows into its mouth and out through gills on either side of its body. Water passing over the gills is rich in oxygen. Blood inside the gill tissues is rich in **carbon dioxide**, a waste product from the fish's body. The blood gives up carbon dioxide and takes oxygen from the water. The water then flows out of the gills, taking the carbon dioxide with it.

Trout live in freshwater lakes and streams.

All fish are a type of animal called a **vertebrate**. Vertebrates have backbones, or spines, made up of many small vertebrae. The backbone is part of a fish's internal skeleton. Some fish have skeletons made of bone. Other fish have skeletons made of **cartilage**, a substance that is not as hard as bone.

All fish have gills for breathing, and most have **fins** for swimming. Some fish are covered with **scales**, but others have none.

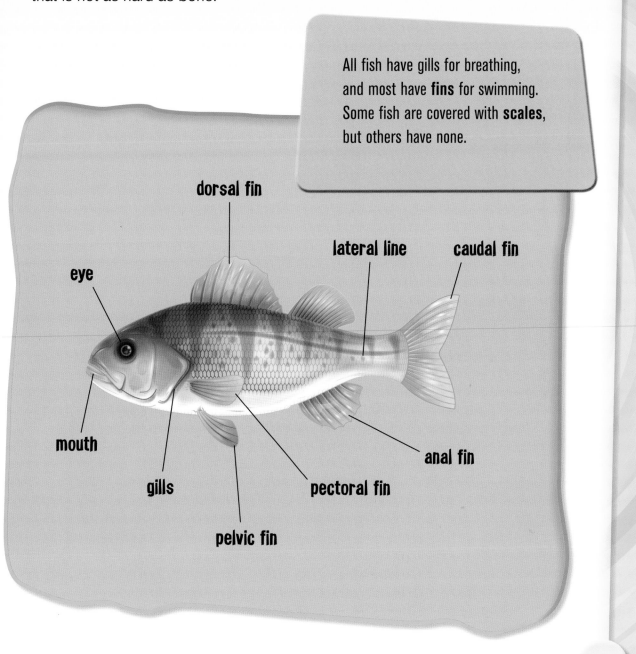

dorsal fin

lateral line

caudal fin

eye

mouth

gills

pelvic fin

pectoral fin

anal fin

Cold-blooded

Most fish are cold-blooded. They cannot control their body temperature. When the water grows colder, the fish cools down. When the water warms up, the fish warms up.

Whether a fish lives in cold or warm water, the fish needs temperatures that are best for it. If a fish gets too cold, it might dive for the bottom. There might be ice on the surface of the water, but the temperature at the bottom is often warmer in winter. Fish that are too cold move more slowly to save their energy. Some fish head south for the winter, if they can swim south down a body of water.

What happens when a fish gets too warm? The fish needs more food and oxygen. If it does not get enough food and oxygen, it will die. The water's bottom might be a good place for the fish to cool down. Heat from the Sun can make the top layers of the water very warm. The water at the bottom stays cooler.

A sailfish has a huge dorsal fin.

Fish that live on **coral reefs** come in many patterns and colors.

Fins for swimming

Most fish have fins. Fish use their fins to swim (see page 5). The dorsal fin on a fish's back and the anal fin on its underside help keep the fish upright in the water. The caudal fin at the end of the tail swings side to side pushing the fish through the water. Pectoral and pelvic fins on each side of the body help a fish steer and turn.

Are There Many Kinds of Fish?

Fish are a huge group of animals. **Biologists** know of more than 25,000 **species**, or types, of fish, and they are still discovering more. Fish make up half of all known **vertebrates**.

Groups of fish

To make sense of the different kinds of fish, scientists classify, or group, fish into two main groups—fish with jaws and fish without jaws. There are many more fish with jaws than without jaws, so scientists have several ways of grouping jawed fish. First they group them into fish that have skeletons made of bone and fish that have skeletons made of **cartilage**.

There are many more fish with bony skeletons, so scientists group the bony fish by the kind of **fins** they have. Almost all the fish in the world have fins with bones, but some fish have fleshy fins (see page 9).

Is a Jellyfish a Fish?

Not all animals with "fish" in their names are really fish. Jellyfish are made of a soft, jellylike material. They do not have bones or fins as fish do, and they belong to an animal group called cnidarians. Shellfish are not fish, either. Shrimp, crabs, and lobsters belong to a group called crustaceans. Crustaceans do not have backbones. Hard outer shells act as external skeletons and protect their bodies. The seahorse, however, is a fish, not a horse! With its long tail and long snout, this creature looks like a horse without legs. It has a backbone, **gills**, and fins.

Jawed fish (more than 25,000 species)

Bony skeleton (more than 24,000 species)	Cartilage skeleton (about 960 species)

Jawless fish (90 species)

Hagfish (50 species)	Lamprey (40 species)

Fleshy-finned (7 species)

Scientists estimate that there are more than 25,000 species of fish. The fish are organized into groups.

Spiny-finned (almost 23,000 species)

Putting Living Things in Groups

Biologists group living things with scientific **classification** systems that go from larger to smaller groups. Fish, for example, are grouped into the large animal kingdom. The next major groups are phylum, class, order, family, genus, and species (the smallest group).

Jawless and jawed

There are only two kinds of jawless fish—lampreys and hagfish. Lampreys have long bodies with fins on their backs. Their backbone is made of cartilage. Lampreys attach to other fish and suck their blood. Lampreys live in freshwater and salt water. Hagfish only live in salt water. They do not have vertebrae. A cord called a notochord runs down their backs.

There are many kinds of jawed fish, which scientists divide into two major groups. One group has bony skeletons, and the other has cartilage skeletons. The cartilage skeleton group is made up of sharks, rays, and chimaeras.

Sharks are fearsome meat eaters.

A lamprey's mouth is like a suction cup with tiny teeth.

Cartilage skeletons

About 460 species of sharks live in oceans all over the world. Sharks are meat-eating fish. They have several rows of teeth that fall out and are replaced with new teeth.

Manta rays, **skates**, stingrays, and other rays look like birds "flying" above the sandy ocean floor. Their "wings" are large pectoral fins on the sides of their flat bodies. There are nearly 500 species of rays.

Chimaeras have large fins on their backs, undersides, and sides. Their bodies taper toward the tail fin. There are fewer than 30 species of chimaeras.

Bony fish

There are more species of bony fish than any other kind. Biologists group bony fish by the kind of fins they have. Some are fleshy-finned and others are spiny-finned.

There are only seven species of fleshy-finned fish. Six species are lungfish. One species is the coelacanth—a fish that has existed since the time of the dinosaurs. Lungfish can breathe with a kind of **lung** when they are out of the water. Some scientists think that vertebrates that live on land may have evolved from lungfish.

Mudskippers are spiny-finned fish that use their pectoral fins like legs to walk across land.

The largest of all groups of fish are the spiny-finned, or ray-finned, fish. Bones that fan out like rays support the fins of these fish. The 23,000 species of spiny-finned fish make up 95 percent of all the world's fish.

Tuna, salmon, perch, and almost all fish that people eat are spiny-finned fish. Some species of spiny-finned fish can also look very unusual.

Sturgeons are huge fish with armored plates instead of **scales**.

A Living Fossil

Biologists once thought that the coelacanth became **extinct** almost 70 million years ago. Some **fossils** of these fish are 300 million years old. Then in 1938, a fisherman caught a coelacanth off South Africa. Since then, about 200 coelacanths have been caught. These brown or blue fish have big tails and strong fins. They can be about 1.8 meters (5.9 feet) long and weigh about 91 kilograms (200 pounds).

How Do Fish Grow?

The life cycle of most fish begins when they hatch from eggs. Some hatch from eggs scattered in the water. Some hatch from eggs attached to wood or other objects. Some hatch from eggs laid in nests made from gravel on a lake bottom. And some hatch from eggs that adults carry in their mouths!

Fish that hatch

Newborn fish are called **larvae**. Young fish are called **fry**. Most adult fish do not take care of their larvae. In fact, the adults of many **species** may accidentally eat their own eggs or larvae.

Some fish species do guard their eggs. Pumpkinseeds and bluegills are small sunfish that live in freshwater lakes and ponds. These fish hatch from eggs that are laid in nests on the bottom of the fresh water. The larvae are tiny, and their bodies are clear. They stay at the bottom of the nest for several days while the male fish guards them.

Some fish species lay large masses of eggs.

These sunfish, like most other larvae, are born with a yolk sac attached to their bodies. The larvae live off of the yolk sac until they develop a mouth. Then the fry are able to eat food.

Born live

Some sharks are born live. These shark eggs develop inside the female's body. The larvae still live off yolk sacs inside the mother shark. The world is a dangerous place for newborn sharks, which are called pups. Like all fish babies, shark pups are in danger of being eaten by bigger fish.

Tiny larvae with big eyes and see-through bodies hatch from eggs.

Fry as food

Fish species lay from just a few eggs to several million eggs. Few fish eggs survive to hatch into larvae. Of these, only a few larvae live to grow into fry, **juvenile** fish, and adult fish.

Some larvae become part of the **plankton** that floats near the surface of freshwater lakes and saltwater oceans. Plankton is made up of tiny organisms, including tiny animals. Many ocean animals, including huge whales, eat plankton.

Many fry become food for other fish, even of their own species. For example, larger flounder fry will eat smaller flounder fry.

A larva hatches from a fish egg, becomes a fry, grows into a juvenile fish, and finally becomes an adult.

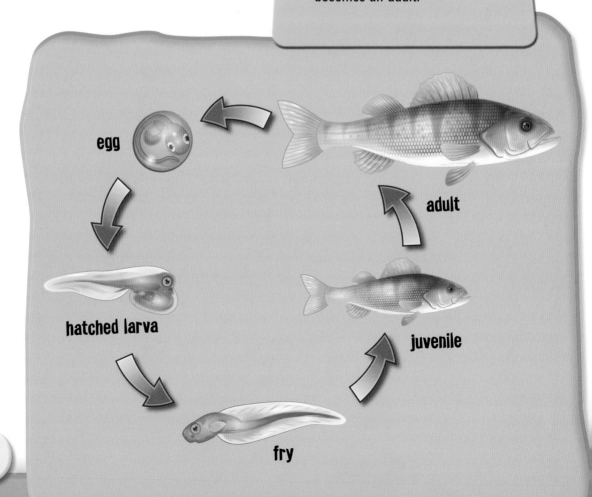

egg

adult

hatched larva

juvenile

fry

A bluegill male guards eggs laid by a female in a nest he built on a lake bottom.

The time it takes for a young fish to grow into an adult depends on its species and its size. Usually small fish become adults more quickly than bigger fish. It takes most bony fish from one to five years to become adults that can **reproduce**. Big sturgeons can take 15 years to become an adult.

How Long Do Fish Live?

Some **coral reef** fish live only a few weeks. Sturgeons can live for more than 50 years. Many fish in **temperate** climates live for 10 to 20 years. To see how old a bony fish is, **biologists** once counted rings that form on fish **scales** every year. Now biologists count rings on ear stones, or otoliths, which are hard structures behind the brain.

Where Do Fish Live?

Fish live in all kinds of water. They live in saltwater oceans. They live in freshwater lakes, ponds, and streams.

Rivers and ponds

Some fish live in the rushing rapids of rivers. Trout often live in rivers with cold, fast-flowing water. Some fish live in quiet ponds. Pike, a game fish prized by people who enjoy the sport of fishing, sometimes lurk in still waters filled with lily pads.

Many kinds of fish, including anchovies, herring, and minnows, spend some or all of their lives in **estuaries**. An estuary is a body of water in which freshwater from a river mixes with ocean water. Ocean tides bring in salt water, which mixes with the freshwater. Chesapeake Bay on the Atlantic Ocean is a big estuary in the United States.

Fish live in all oceans, which cover almost 70 percent of Earth's surface.

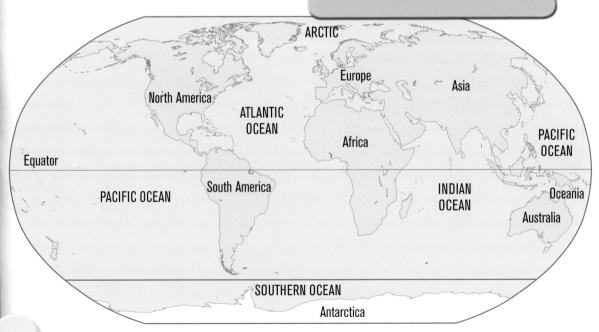

Fresh and salty water

Some fish live part of their lives in freshwater and part of their lives in salt water. Salmon hatch from eggs laid in freshwater rivers and streams. When they become adults, the salmon travel down rivers to the ocean.

Coral Reefs

The hard skeletons of tiny animals, mainly corals, build up reefs in tropical seas. Living corals come in many shapes and colors, as do the fish that live there. Parrotfish can be yellow, blue, and green. The Moorish idol has black, white, and yellow stripes.

Orange and white clown fish live on reefs among the stinging tentacles of the sea **anemone**.

Cold water

Some fish live in icy cold waters. Winter water temperatures in the **Arctic** Ocean near the North Pole fall to −2°C (28°F). Water is equally cold in the waters around **Antarctica**.

Many fish **species** in Antarctica and cod in the Arctic have a kind of **antifreeze** in their blood. The antifreeze **adaptation** developed in these fish when the climates changed from warm to cold, millions of years ago.

Arctic cod can live in ice water because it has a kind of antifreeze in its blood.

Piranhas use their sharp teeth for eating all kinds of animals during the Amazon rain forest's dry season.

Warm water

Many kinds of unusual fish live in the warm waters of Africa and South America. The elephant nose fish lives in Africa's Congo River system. It has a long snout that looks like the trunk of an elephant!

Piranhas live in lakes and rivers in South America. During the dry season, food is scarce because the water in rivers and ponds dries up. Piranhas use their sharp teeth and powerful jaws to tear flesh from even larger animals that are struggling. Tiger fish that live in the Congo River also have sharp teeth and behave in much the same way as piranhas do.

Bioluminescence

Organisms that can give off their own light are called bioluminescent. Many bioluminescent creatures live in the deep sea. There are about 1,000 species of bioluminescent fish. Lanternfish use bioluminescence to communicate and to attract **prey**.

Shallow and deep water

Some fish can live in just a few inches of freshwater or salt water. Other fish live so deep in the ocean that sunlight cannot reach them. Freshwater fish such as pike and perch live at different levels of lakes and streams depending on the weather.

Fish live at every level of the ocean. Some fish live near the ocean surface, hundreds of miles from shore. These fish are big and can swim very fast. Bonito, mackerel, marlin, swordfish, blue sharks, and tuna are some fish that live near the surface of the open ocean.

Gulper eels have long bodies and huge mouths. **Biologists** think they use their mouths as a net to catch small animals in the deep sea.

Many kinds of fish live midway between the top and bottom of the ocean. In this midwater, there is not enough sunlight for plants to grow. Midwater fish swim to the top at night to feed on **plankton**.

The deep ocean is pitch-black. Sunlight never reaches the deep ocean bottom. Strange-looking fish live there. The deep-sea anglerfish dangles a glowing lure from a spine on its nose. It catches animals that come near its sharp teeth.

Pupfish

Small pupfish live in desert springs and pools in the southwestern United States and Mexico. In winter pupfish burrow into mud at the water's bottom to keep warm. In summer pupfish can live in water that is as hot as 42°C (108°F).

The deep-sea anglerfish dangles a bioluminescent lure to attract its dinner.

How Do Fish Spend Their Time?

Some fish spend most of their time with other fish. Fierce hunters, such as great white sharks, are usually alone. Some small fish spend time helping bigger fish. The cleaner wrasse eats **parasites** that grow on the mouth and **gills** of big fish.

Swimming long distances

Fish have different ways of swimming. Sharks swish their powerful tails. Eels wave their snakelike bodies back and forth. Rays flap their big **fins** like wings as they glide just above the ocean floor.

A school of tuna swims together in the open ocean.

What Are Schools of Fish?

Schools of fish have nothing to do with learning lessons. Schools of fish are groups that live together. Some schools are small and others are large. Tuna form small schools with as few as 25 fish. A herring school can have many millions of fish. All the individual fish in a school are about the same size. Some fish form a school when they are **juveniles**. They stay in the same school all of their lives.

Many fish spend a great deal of time **migrating**. Some fish travel hundreds of miles from one place to another. Fish usually migrate when they **breed**. American and European eels, for example, migrate to and from an area of the Atlantic Ocean called the Sargasso Sea.

Great white sharks that live along the California coast migrate once a year to Hawaii. Bluefin tuna living off Ireland migrate thousands of miles to both sides of the Atlantic Ocean.

A shark pursues its **prey**.

Resting

Fish need to spend time resting from daily activities. **Biologists** are not sure if fish sleep in the way that people and other mammals do. Except for sharks, most fish do not have eyelids, so they cannot close their eyes to sleep.

Fish that are active during the day rest quietly at night. Reef fish, for example, dart to and fro all day long. At night they hide from **predators** in cracks and caves in the coral. Some fish are active at night. Many kinds of catfish eat at night and rest during the day. Perch and other freshwater fish float under logs or other structures during the day and at night.

Sharks and rays swim all the time. They swim even while they rest. Unlike other fish, these sharks cannot pump water containing **oxygen** over their gills. They must swim to keep water flowing through their gill slits.

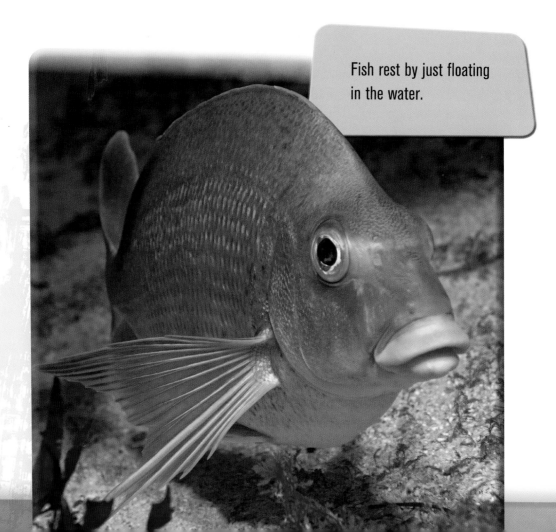

Fish rest by just floating in the water.

Lungfish go into a sleeplike state called estivation during dry, hot summers.

Estivating and hibernating

Some fish spend hot, dry seasons in a state called **estivation**. This means they stay in one place. These fish live in desert streams, ponds, and other places where water dries up in summer. African lungfish make a kind of cocoon when they estivate. They burrow into the mud to keep from drying out.

Antarctic cod drop to the seafloor and slow down during cold winters. They go into a state like hibernation in land animals. Hibernation is like a deep sleep.

What Do Fish Eat?

Fish eat different kinds of things at different stages in their life cycle. Fish **fry** eat **algae** and **plankton**. They help keep the amount of algae and plankton under control in lakes.

Fish food webs

The fry and small fish become food for bigger fish. Bigger fish help keep the numbers of these smaller fish under control. Fish are very important in the balance of nature in freshwater and saltwater **ecosystems**.

Every fish plays an important part in the ecosystem.

Plant eaters

Some adult fish only eat algae. Parrotfish that live around **coral reefs** in tropical oceans mainly eat algae. They have strong front teeth that look like a parrot's beak. Parrotfish use their beaks to break off and grind up coral. One parrotfish grinds enough coral to produce 90 kilograms (200 pounds) of sand a year!

Some **species** of carp are freshwater herbivores. Carp are native to places in Asia. The grass carp and Asian carp were brought to the United States from Asia to solve a problem. Plants were clogging some bodies of water. The plan was to have the carp eat the plants. The number of carp grew rapidly, however. The carp became a threat to other freshwater fish.

This parrotfish displays its strong front teeth.

Meat eaters

Most fish are meat eaters, or carnivores. Freshwater pike and perch will eat anything except plants. Pike eat smaller fish, insects, frogs, small birds, and mammals. Lungfish eat frogs and snails as well as small fish.

A large fish eats a smaller one.

Do Sharks Eat People?

More than 40 kinds of sharks, including tiger sharks, nurse sharks, bull sharks, mako sharks, and hammerheads have attacked people. The attacks can cause serious injuries. The most feared sharks are the great whites, which have caused deaths. **Biologists** are not sure why sharks attack. Great whites could mistake people for other sea animals, such as seals or sea lions.

Ocean fish, such as tuna and cod, eat smaller fish and squid. Cod also eat shellfish. Flounders eat fish and shrimp. Rays use their blunt teeth to crush the shells of clams, oysters, and shellfish that live on the seafloor. Eels eat small fish and octopus.

All sharks are carnivores. They have a keen (sharp) sense of smell and hearing. Most sharks grab smaller fish and other **prey** with their razor-sharp teeth. The bigger the shark, the bigger the fish they eat. Great white sharks will eat birds and sea lions. There are exceptions to this rule. Huge whale sharks and **megamouths** mainly eat plankton. Whale sharks are the biggest fish alive.

Tips for Avoiding Shark Attacks

- Never go in the water with a bleeding sore or cut. Blood attracts sharks.
- Head for the beach immediately if a shark is spotted.
- Stay away from large groups of seabirds, dolphins, or other sea animals.
- Do not swim near fishing boats.
- Do not swim at night or in muddy water.
- Never swim alone.

What Eats Fish?

Fish are an important food for many kinds of animals, including mammals and birds, as well as other fish. Fish are an important food for people, too. Fish are good sources of **protein**, vitamins, and minerals.

Mammals

Some mammals that live in the **Arctic** and in **Antarctica** eat fish. Weddell seals of Antarctica go ice fishing. They use their mouths to make a hole in the ice. Then they dive deep into the cold water to catch a fish dinner.

Bears of the western United States add fish to their menu during the summer months. Bears are omnivores, which means they eat plants and animals. The grizzlies that live around Yellowstone National Park catch trout. The favorite food of grizzlies and other brown bears, however, is salmon. Every summer and fall, salmon swim from the ocean up rivers to lay their eggs. The bears are waiting to snag them out of the rivers.

A grizzly bear uses its big paw to snatch a salmon from the rushing river water.

Birds

Birds that live near oceans, lakes, and rivers eat fish. Eagles swoop down to catch injured fish floating on the surface of northern lakes. Gulls that live on lake and ocean shores circle above the water until they spot a tasty looking fish near the surface. Pelicans use their big bills like fishing nets and fill them with small saltwater fish. Long-legged wading birds, such as the great blue heron or the wood stork, search for fish in the shallow waters of ponds and marshes.

A pelican scoops up a fish with his bill.

Food for people

People eat a lot of fish. People who live in Asian countries eat the most fish. People who live in certain parts of Africa eat the least amount of fish.

Most of the fish that people eat comes from the ocean. Fishing boats catch tons of ocean fish in big nets. Some of the fish comes from fish farms. Fish farmers care for these fish throughout their life cycle, from eggs to **fry** to adult fish. People also eat fish that they catch for sport.

These fish tumble from a net into the hold of a commercial fishing boat.

You can buy fresh fish to eat right away. You can buy frozen fish to eat another day. You can buy cans of salmon and tuna that will keep for many months.

People use fish for products other than food. Factories make some fish into **fertilizer**. Factories make some fish into food for animals.

Fishing boats all over the world catch more than 80 million tons of fish a year. Some people worry that too many fish are being caught. They worry that there will not be enough adult fish left to lay eggs and **reproduce**. This could make the number of fish all over the world drop very low.

Nutrients in Fish

Fish has almost as much protein as meat. Fish also have special fats that are good for heart health. Researchers have found that omega-3 fatty acids in salmon and other fatty fish help prevent heart disease.

How Do Fish Protect Themselves?

Fish often face many dangers, including hungry enemies. Fish, however, have many ways of protecting themselves. Some fish hide. Others put on wonderful disguises. Some fish have ways of fighting back. Still other fish use "bodyguards" for protection!

Blending and bluffing

The flat bodies of **skates**, rays, and flounders have colors and patterns on their skin. This protective coloration helps them blend in with the sandy ocean bottom.

Puffer fish are as small as 5 centimeters (2 inches). When a **predator** comes along, the puffer gulps water to expand its stomach. It can blow up to twice its size to frighten its enemies.

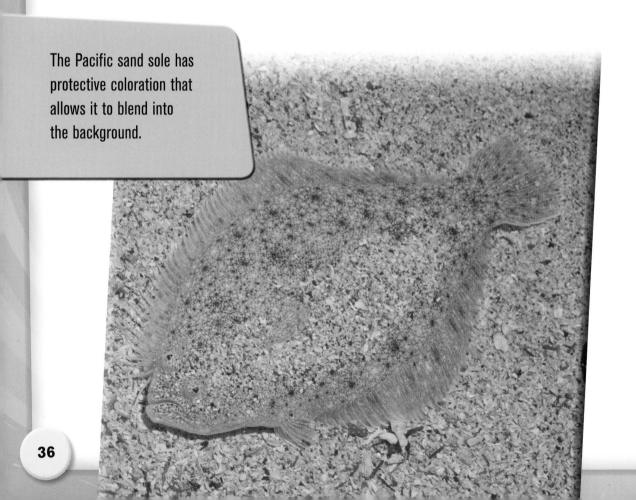

The Pacific sand sole has protective coloration that allows it to blend into the background.

Porcupine fish also swallow enough water to expand to twice their size. Their bodies are covered with sharp, stiff spines that lie flat until the fish is scared. Then the spines stick up like the quills of a porcupine.

Other protections

Catfish have spines that can stab into the skin of anything that attacks. The spines give off a poison that can injure a predator.

Primitive fish that have been around since the days of the dinosaurs have protective "armor." Sturgeons have tough skin and hard, bony plates that protect their long, slender bodies.

The tiny orange and white clown fish has a bodyguard. It lives among the stinging tentacles of the sea **anemone**. The clown fish cleans the anemone. It has a coating that protects it from the anemone's tentacles.

A stingray hides by burrowing into the sand.

Releasing poisons

Some fish release poisons called venom. **Biologists** have counted about 1,200 kinds of venomous fish. There are more venomous fish than venomous snakes!

Most venomous fish live in the **tropics**. The graceful lionfish has a red and white striped body and pectoral **fins** that wave like feathers in the water. It also has 18 dorsal fins that are sharp as needles and deliver a powerful venom.

Some fish cause animals that eat them to get sick or die. The organs of puffer fish contain a deadly poison. People in Japan eat puffer fish, which they call fugu. Specially trained cooks know how to prepare fugu safely.

When the porcupine fish makes itself bigger by gulping water, spines stick out all over its body.

Fighting or fleeing

Surgeonfish have sharp spines near their tails. The spines can cause deep cuts in anything that grabs them, including people. Some surgeonfish, such as the yellow tang and the blue tang, are very beautiful.

Some fish can swim very fast to escape predators. Flying fish beat their tail fins to gather enough speed to leap out of the water. They spread their pectoral fins like wings to glide over the surface. These fish can "fly" as high as 1.2 meters (3.9 feet) and travel as far as 200 meters (655 feet)!

Deadly Stonefish

Stonefish hide themselves in sand. Their rough, grayish brown bodies look like stones as they wait for **prey**. Spines on their fins give off a powerful venom. A stonefish can kill a person who steps on it.

How Do Fish Have Babies?

Fish **reproduce** sexually. Sperm from a male joins with eggs from a female. The sperm **fertilizes** the egg. The egg hatches into a new fish.

There are two main ways that fertilization takes place. One way is called spawning. The other way is called mating.

Eggs from spawning

Spawning is also called external fertilization. Sperm join with eggs outside the female's body. The female releases eggs into the water as the male releases sperm. Most bony fish reproduce by spawning.

Most fish have spawning seasons. Fish that live in cold water usually spawn in fall or winter. Fish that live in places where there are four seasons usually spawn in spring or early summer. Tropical fish can spawn at any time of the year.

A female releases eggs into the water to be fertilized by sperm.

Fish usually return to the same place to spawn. Some fish must travel long distances to their spawning grounds. Salmon may travel 3,200 kilometers (2,000 miles) from the Pacific Ocean up a certain river. European eels travel up to 5,000 kilometers (3,100 miles) from rivers in Europe to the Sargasso Sea. The Sargasso Sea is an area of the North Atlantic Ocean that is filled with floating seaweed.

Some fish gather in groups of many thousands to spawn. Other fish, such as salmon, spawn in pairs.

Fish Ladders

Dams on rivers block the way of salmon swimming upstream to spawn. To help the salmon get over the dams, engineers build sloping fish ladders. Fish ladders are like waterfalls with steps. The salmon jump from one step to another to get over the dam.

Eggs from mating

Mating is also called internal fertilization. The male releases sperm to fertilize eggs inside the female fish. Sharks, rays, and chimaeras mate. A few bony fish, such as guppies and scorpion fish, also reproduce by mating.

After mating, **skates** and some kinds of sharks release fertilized eggs into the water. These fish do not guard or care for their eggs. Each egg has a tough covering called a mermaid's purse. The covering protects the egg.

In other fish that mate, the eggs develop inside the fish. The unhatched fish, or embryos, get food from a yolk sac. The female then gives birth to live babies. Most rays, guppies, and some scorpion fish give birth to live young. **Hammerheads**, bull sharks, lemon sharks, and mako sharks are some **species** that give birth to live shark pups. The parent sharks, however, do not care for the newborn pups.

All fish produced from mating are born able to care for themselves. Sharks that hatch from eggs in the water have teeth and can swim. Rays and sharks that are born live are also fully developed.

Cannibal Shark Babies

The eggs of some sharks, including sand tiger sharks, develop inside the female. When the eggs hatch in the mother shark, they must take care of themselves. Unlike hammerheads and some other sharks, the mother's body does not provide food for the babies. So the strongest newly hatched sharks eat their weaker brothers and sisters.

A shark gives birth to live babies.

Fish Facts

The largest fish in the world is the whale shark.

The smallest known fish include the stout infantfish of Australia's Great Barrier Reef at 7 millimeters (0.28 inch) long, and the Paedocypris of Sumatra at 7.9 millimeters (0.3 inch).

There are more bristlemouths than any other kind of fish. Billions of these tiny fish live in the ocean.

The black swallower, which grows to about 25.4 centimeters (10 inches), has hinged jaws that allow it to swallow animals more than twice its size.

The deepest-dwelling fish yet found is a snailfish living 8 kilometers (5 miles) deep in the ocean off Japan.

Many kinds of fish, such as clown fish, change genders during their lifetimes. Some change from males to females. Others change from females to males. Sometimes the changes occur due to shifts in the environment or the fish community.

Male seahorses carry **fertilized** eggs in a pouch on their abdomens.

Tiny **juvenile** eels with clear bodies are called glass eels before they develop into larger eels.

The huge and rare **megamouth** shark was first discovered in 1976 off Hawaii. Despite its big mouth and 50 rows of tiny teeth, this rare fish feeds on small sea animals called krill.

The fish eggs of Russian sturgeons have caused the **species** to become endangered. The eggs are sold as an expensive dish called caviar.

Electric eels, which are not true eels, generate electric charges that are powerful enough to kill fish or stun people.

Many fish are light colored on their bellies and dark colored on their backs. The colors make them hard to see from below and hard to see from above.

Schools of many small fish can provide protection for themselves by tricking enemies into thinking the school is one big fish.

Glossary

adaptation change that makes a species better suited to its environment

alga (pl. algae) small plant or plantlike organism

anemone sea creature that does not move and has stinging tentacles around its mouth

Antarctica region around the South Pole

antifreeze substance that lowers the freezing temperature of a liquid

Arctic region around the North Pole

biologist scientist who studies living things

breed to produce offspring

carbon dioxide gas in the air that is a waste product of animal respiration and needed by plants

cartilage tough, flexible tissue that makes up the skeletons of sharks and some other fish

classification system for grouping things

coral reef stony underwater structure made from the skeletons of sea animals

ecosystem community of living organisms as well as their nonliving environment

estivation animal's sleeplike state during dry, hot weather

estuary wide mouth of a river where salt and freshwater mix

extinct no longer in existence

fertilize adding male sperm to make a female egg develop into a new individual

fertilizer substance added to soil to help plants grow

fin body part on fish that enables them to swim

fossil remains of an organism from the past or its image saved in rock

fry early stage in the life cycle of fish

gill organ in fish that enables blood to take oxygen from water and give up carbon dioxide (a waste product)

juvenile young animal

larva (pl. larvae) early form of a fish that hatches from an egg

lung organ in land animals that enables blood to take oxygen from air and give up carbon dioxide (a waste product)

megamouth species of shark with a huge mouth

migrate move from one place to another with the change of seasons

oxygen gas found in air that animals need to breathe

parasite animal or plant that lives on another living thing

plankton small animals that float in water

predator animal that hunts and eats another animal

prey animal hunted for food

protein substance that is part of muscles and bones and is found in some foods

reproduce to produce offspring

scale small, hard plate that protects the skin of some fish

skate large fish with a diamond-shaped body

species group of living things that have similar traits and can breed

temperate mild climate without extreme hot or cold temperatures

tropics regions north or south of Earth's equator

vertebrate animal with a backbone

Find Out More

Books

Crossingham, John. *The Life Cycle of a Shark*. New York: Crabtree, 2005.

Lundblad, Kristina, and Bobbie Kalman. *Animals Called Fish*. New York: Crabtree, 2005.

Schulte, Mary. *Piranhas and Other Fish*. New York: Children's Press, 2005.

Sexton, Colleen. *The Life Cycle of a Salmon*. Minneapolis: Bellwether Media, 2010.

Websites

Fish Frequently Asked Questions
www.nefsc.noaa.gov/faq/

National Geographic Kids: Creature Features
http://kids.nationalgeographic.com/kids/animals/creaturefeature

San Diego Natural History Museum: Shark School
www.sdnhm.org/kids/sharks/index.html

Index